W9-BYY-061

Growing Readers

New Hanover County Public Library

Purchased with
New Hanover County Partnership for Children
and Smart Start Funds

DISCARDED
New Hanover from County Public Library

SandCastle 2

The Senses

Sense of Hearing

Carey Molter

ABDO
Publishing Company

NEW HANOVER COUNTY
PUBLIC LIBRARY
201 CHESTNUT STREET
WILMINGTON, N C 28401

Published by SandCastle™, an imprint of ABDO Publishing Company, 4940 Viking Drive, Edina, Minnesota 55435.

Copyright © 2001 by Abdo Consulting Group, Inc. International copyrights reserved in all countries. No part of this book may be reproduced in any form without written permission from the publisher. SandCastle™ is a trademark and logo of Abdo Publishing Company.

Printed in the United States.

Photo credits: Comstock, Corbis Images, Corel, Eyewire Images, Image 100, PhotoDisc, Rubberball

Library of Congress Cataloging-in-Publication Data

Molter, Carey, 1973-
    Sense of hearing / Carey Molter.
        p. cm. -- (The senses)
    Includes index.
    ISBN 1-57765-627-X
    1. Hearing--Juvenile literature. [1. Hearing 2. Senses and sensation.] I. Title.

QP462.2 .M64 2001
612.8'5--dc21
                                                    2001022900

The SandCastle concept, content, and reading method have been reviewed and approved by a national advisory board including literacy specialists, librarians, elementary school teachers, early childhood education professionals, and parents.

Let Us Know

After reading the book, SandCastle would like you to tell us your stories about reading. What is your favorite page? Was there something hard that you needed help with? Share the ups and downs of learning to read. We want to hear from you! To get posted on the Abdo Publishing Company Web site, send us email at:

sandcastle@abdopub.com

About SandCastle™

Nonfiction books for the beginning reader

- Basic concepts of phonics are incorporated with integrated language methods of reading instruction. Most words are short, and phrases, letter sounds, and word sounds are repeated.

- Readability is determined by the number of words in each sentence, the number of characters in each word, and word lists based on curriculum frameworks.

- Full-color photography reinforces word meanings and concepts.

- "Words I Can Read" list at the end of each book teaches basic elements of grammar, helps the reader recognize the words in the text, and builds vocabulary.

- Reading levels are indicated by the number of flags on the castle.

Look for more SandCastle books in these three reading levels:

Level 1 (one flag)	**Level 2** (two flags)	**Level 3** (three flags)
SandCastle 1	SandCastle 2	SandCastle 3
Grades Pre-K to K 5 or fewer words per page	**Grades K to 1** 5 to 10 words per page	**Grades 1 to 2** 10 to 15 words per page

Our senses tell us what
is going on around us.

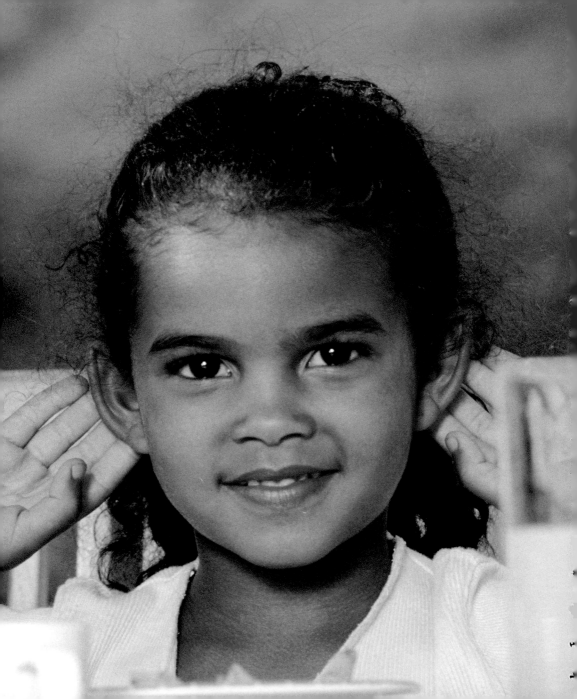

Hearing is one of our five senses.

Hearing helps us know what something sounds like.

The sound of a rooster
wakes me up.

Some sounds are soft.

Rain on our umbrella is quiet.

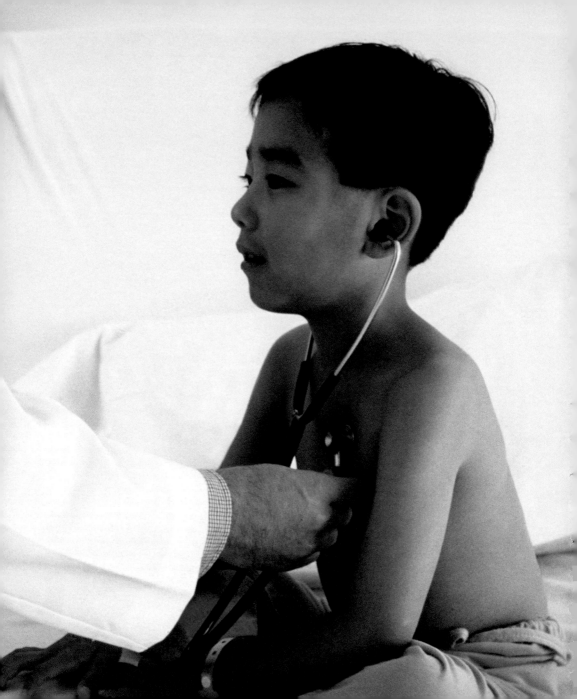

Sometimes we need help
to hear a quiet sound.

Some noises mean danger.

They help keep us safe.

Noisemakers are also loud.

They squeak and quack!

What sounds do you think they hear?

Words I Can Read

Nouns
A noun is a person, place, or thing

danger (DAYN-JUR) p. 17

hearing
  (HIHR-ing) pp. 7, 9

help (HELP) p. 15

rain (RAYN) p. 13

rooster (ROO-stur) p. 11

sound
  (SOUND) pp. 11, 15

umbrella
  (uhm-BREL-uh) p. 13

Plural Nouns
A plural noun is more than one
person, place, or thing

noisemakers
  (NOIZ-make-urz) p. 19

noises (NOIZ-ez) p. 17

senses (SENSS-ez) pp. 5, 7

sounds
  (SOUNDZ) pp. 13, 21

Verbs

A verb is an action or being word

are (AR) pp. 13, 19

do (DOO) p. 21

going (GOH-ing) p. 5

hear (HIHR) pp. 15, 21

help (HELP) p. 17

helps (HELPSS) p. 9

is (IZ) pp. 5, 7, 13

keep (KEEP) p. 17

know (NOH) p. 9

mean (MEEN) p. 17

need (NEED) p. 15

quack (KWAK) p. 19

sounds (SOUNDZ) p. 9

squeak (SKWEEK) p. 19

tell (TEL) p. 5

think (THINGK) p. 21

wakes (WAYKSS) p. 11

Adjectives

An adjective describes something

five (FIVE) p. 7

loud (LOUD) p. 19

one (WUHN) pp. 7, 21

quiet
  (KWYE-uht) pp. 13, 15

safe (SAYF) p. 17

soft (SAWFT) p. 13

some (SUHM) pp. 13, 17

23

More About the Sense of Hearing
Match the Words to their Pictures

clap

ring

rattle

whisper

Growing Readers
New Hanover County
Public Library
201 Chestnut Street
Wilmington, NC 28401

6/02

Bag